World Religions

HINDUISM

Ranchor Prime

WALRUS
B O O K S

WORLD RELIGIONS

BUDDHISM   CHRISTIANITY   HINDUISM   ISLAM   JUDAISM   SIKHISM

Library and Archives Canada Cataloguing in Publication

Prime, Ranchor, 1950-
          Hinduism / Ranchor Prime.
(World religions)

ISBN 1-55285-655-0

          1. Hinduism--Juvenile literature. I. Title. II. Series: World religions (North Vancouver, B.C.)

BL1203.P75 2005   j294.5   C2004-906016-3

Editorial Manager: Joyce Bentley	Senior Editor: Sarah Nunn
Project Editor: Lionel Bender	Text Editors: Michael March
Designer: Richard Johnson	Art Editor: Ben White
Proofreader: Jennifer Smart	Indexer: Peter Harrison

Cover Make-up: Mike Spender, Additional Design
Diagrams and maps: Stefan Chabluk
Picture Researchers: Joanne O'Brien at Circa Photo Library, and Cathy Stastny
Produced by Bender Richardson White, PO Box 266, Uxbridge, UB9 5NX, U.K.

Thanks to Joanne O'Brien at ICOREC, Manchester, U.K. for planning the structure and content of these books. Thanks, too, to Hindu Consultant Rasamandala Das, a practicing member of the Vaishnava tradition. He runs an educational consultancy in Oxford and is co-director of ISKCON Educational Services.

The Publisher acknowledges the financial support of the Government of Canada through the Book Publishing Industry Development Program for our publishing activities.

Printed and bound in China

Picture Acknowledgments
We wish to thank the following individuals and organizations for their help and assistance, and for supplying material in their collections: Circa Photo Library: pages 9, 11, 46; (Bipinchandra J. Mistry) cover, 1, 5 top, 6, 10, 17, 18, 22, 40, 48–49, 54–55; (William Holtby) 5 center, 8, 14, 29, 31, 34, 39, 47; (John Smith) 4, 5 bottom, 7, 12, 13, 15, 16, 25, 26, 28, 50–51; (Christine Osborne) 20, 23, 27, 30, 35; (Robyn Beeche) 24; (Ged Murray) 38. Corbis Images: (Michael A. Koller Studio Ltd) 19; (David H. Wells) 32, 45; (Adam Woolfitt) 37. Ranchor Prime: 11, 42, 43, 52–53. Topham Photo Library: (Picturepoint) 33; (TheImage Works/Mitch Wojnarowicz) 36; (Universal Pictorial Press Photo) 41; (PressNet) 44. The pictures used in this book do not show the actual people named in the case studies in the text.

CONTENTS

Sanjay's Story

Sanjay Chandaria, who is 15, and his sister Anita, 17, live with their parents in Leicester, England. Their grandmother, who also lives with the family, goes a Hindu temple every day, and has taught Sanjay and Anita all they know about the Hindu religion.

"MY PARENTS AND grandmother came to England in 1972 as refugees from Uganda, in East Africa, when the Asian community was expelled. They arrived with only three suitcases and had to start their lives all over again. My older sister, who used to live with us, recently married a doctor who, like us, is a Hindu. The couple now live in the U.S.A., in Washington, D.C.

My grandmother exercises her matriarchal influence over the home. She made sure my sisters and I were brought up as vegetarians and taught about Hinduism, by telling us stories when we were little, and teaching us songs to sing at the temple.

I like going to the temple. I can meet my friends there and we all get on really well together. I also have other friends, from other parts of the community, because people in Leicester enjoy a very multicultural life. There are lots of opportunities to meet people at school and college, and around the city.

When I finish my studies, I hope to go into partnership with some of my friends to start our own business. I want to do business because it's something I have a natural talent for. It's my family tradition to be merchants. If I'm successful, I will use my money to support the community. I also want to travel to Gujarat, in India, to see the village that my family originally came from.

My sister, Anita, wants to be a lawyer. She strongly believes in people's right to freedom. People should not be made to suffer from other people's prejudice, she says, as our parents suffered when they first arrived from East Africa. They now consider themselves lucky to be living in a free society. That is why Anita wants to work as a lawyer. There are so many rights we must protect, she says.

To be successful in life, you have to believe in what you are doing, and make yourself your own message by setting a good example. I think my Hindu faith has influenced my views, because I was brought up with a clear moral code that I believe in. But I do not expect everyone to be like me. Hinduism is very open-minded and accepts people the way they are. It has taught me to respect all people and to see all religions as paths to the same ultimate truth."

Hindus across the world

The number of Hindus worldwide is estimated at 850 million, of whom 800 million live in India.

SOUTHEAST ASIA
Hindu nurses – one with her son – in Varanasi, India. Hinduism started in India. In former times, India established trade connections throughout southeast Asia, with Hindu merchants settling in Burma, Malaysia, and Indonesia.

GREAT BRITAIN
A convert to Hinduism at a temple in Manchester. In the late 1700s, India came under British rule. Hindus were encouraged to emigrate to other parts of the British Empire. Many of them went to Britain, allowing people there to convert to the faith.

NORTH AMERICA
A student from the U.S.A. who has converted to Hinduism. After 1945, most Hindus who left India emigrated to Canada, the United States, New Zealand, and Australia. There, people of other faiths have been attracted to the Hindu ways of living.

What Is Hinduism?

The word "Hindu" comes from the River Sindhu, or Indus, which flows across the northwest plains of India. Invaders who crossed the river named the land and the people after the river. A more accurate name for Hinduism is Sanatan Dharma, which means "the eternal truth of life."

"SANATAN DHARMA" DESCRIBES the essential quality that unites all living things – human, animal, and vegetable – with the universe that surrounds them and, ultimately, with God, the source of their existence. It is the belief in the unity of all life that causes Hindus to resist separating their own faith from the other great faith traditions of the world. To a Hindu, all religions are part of the process of discovering the unity of God, humanity, and nature.

A priest reads from the scriptures while devotees bathe in the River Ganges. For Hindus, the ultimate purpose of life is to realize God.

What do Hindus believe?

At the heart of Hinduism is a belief in an eternal spiritual truth, called Brahman, from whom all existence comes. The purpose of life, Hindus say, is to understand this truth and to understand our own spiritual identity as the eternal *atma*, or soul. This soul passes through many kinds of life, but only human life offers the chance to learn this truth. It is therefore important to use the opportunity of a human birth, Hindus believe, to understand who we are, and who God is. In this way, we can end the cycle of reincarnation (rebirth) and be reunited with the eternal spiritual reality, or God.

A child sells devotional statues at Diwali festival time. Hindus believe that all work produces a karmic reaction, but when work is devoted to God it brings freedom from the cycle of rebirth.

What is reincarnation?

Hindus believe that the soul is eternal and lives many lifetimes, in one body after another. Being reborn in a new body is called reincarnation. The soul is sometimes born in a human body, sometimes in an animal body, and sometimes in a plant body, such as a tree. All forms of life contain a soul, and all souls have the chance to experience life in different forms. The cycle of rebirth is called *samsara*. It gives rise to the basic problems of material life, which are birth, disease, old age, and death.

What is karma and why does it matter?

Karma is the Sanskrit word for "action." Actions are important because they produce reactions. Everything that we experience, Hindus say, pleasant or

The Wheel of Rebirth

Under the influence of karma, the soul moves upward and downward on the wheel of rebirth. Hinduism teaches that the ultimate solution to life's basic problems is to be released from your karma, and gain freedom from the cycle of birth and rebirth.

unpleasant, is linked to our past actions in this lifetime or in some previous lifetime, whether or not we see the connections. This does not mean there is no free choice, because we can choose to change our actions, and so change our future. Belief in karma teaches us to accept responsibility for our behavior, and learn from our mistakes.

The "Supreme" is revered in the hearts of all living beings as the "supersoul," called Paramatma.

Vishnu enters the human world in every age to teach us the path of religion and to show his love. Vishnu's incarnations as Rama and Krishna are particularly important to Hindus.

Besides these primary forms of God, there are other divine forms, called *devas* (or demi-gods), empowered by God to govern the forces of nature, such as the planets and the elements. Examples include Agni, the god of fire; Vayu, god of the wind; Surya, god of the sun; and the goddess Ganga, spirit of the Ganges River. Hindus honour God directly, in the personal forms of Krishna, Rama, Vishnu, and Shiva, or in indirectly in divine forms of nature, such as fire, wind, and sun.

Do Hindus believe in many gods?

Hindus believe in one "Supreme Truth," which manifests itself in many forms. God exists as the original creator of the universe, as its maintainer, and as its ultimate destroyer. These three functions are personified in the deities of Brahma the Creator, Vishnu the Preserver, and Shiva the Destroyer. Another important aspect of the "Supreme" is the goddess Devi, who appears in different forms to accompany the different aspects of God.

Why so many stories about Hindu gods?

Stories are important because they impart the traditional wisdom embedded in them. Stories are easier to remember than sermons or philosophy,

The striking form of Shiva dancing in a circle of flames depicts the time, at the end of the universe, when his dance of destruction burns everything to ashes.

but can be just as profound. They are accessible to everyone because they can be communicated by song, drama, or dance, and have a big influence on their audience.

One of the most powerful Hindu stories is the epic *Ramayana*, about how Rama rescued his wife Sita, and dedicated himself to the good of his people. Another joyful and profound story is of Krishna, who lived in the forest as a cowherd in his youth and later became a prince. Krishna taught the *Bhagavad Gita*, perhaps the best summary of Hindu teachings.

DEBATE – Should we believe in an eternal spiritual reality?

- No. There is no proof of a spiritual existence. We should just believe in what we can see. Religion is just an escape from reality.
- Yes. Throughout history, humans have chosen to believe in a spiritual reality beyond this world. Just because we cannot see or hear something, does not mean it does not exist. It is reasonable to believe in other forms of existence besides our own.

How Did Hinduism Begin?

Hinduism has no single founder and is too old to have any historical foundation. Its origins go back way beyond the beginnings of recorded history.

THE TRADITIONS AND teachings of Hinduism were passed down orally from one generation to the next, until they began to be written down in their present Sanskrit form during the second millennium B.C.E. According to these ancient traditions, Krishna lived around 3000 B.C.E., and Rama tens of thousands of years before Krishna.

How were the teachings preserved?

The early teachings of Hinduism were recorded in verse form, so that they could more easily be committed to memory. Early Hindu teachers thought dependence on writing was a sign of weak memory. They preferred to memorize everything and taught their disciples in the same way. The early hymns were collected into four groups, the *Rig, Sama, Yajur,* and *Atharva,* which together are called the four *Vedas.* Later came other texts, such as the Puranas (the old stories), the *Ramayana,* and the *Mahabharata,* which includes the popular *Bhagavad Gita.*

Hindu traditions are passed from one generation to another, at such meeting places as Varanasi, where the faithful gather to bathe in the Ganges River.

Sanskrit, the oldest philosophical language

Sanskrit is written using an alphabet called Devanagari, which means "the language of the gods." Hindus believe that Sanskrit is written and spoken by the *devas*, who live in heavenly realms above the earth. Although the Hindu scriptures are translated into other languages besides Sanskrit, anyone who wants to study them intensely learns Sanskrit. The best- known Sanskrit word is *Om*, meaning "Supreme Truth." It is made up of three letters, A-U-M, and is written like this

A page from a manuscript of the Ramayana, *showing Rama and Sita in the forest.*

What is the system of Hindu teaching?

The core of Hindu teachings is "disciplic succession." This means that the teachings are passed from one generation to another through a system of discipleship and obedience.

When a disciple has passed the tests set by the teacher, he or she can learn the secrets of the Vedic teaching – the wisdom descended from the Vedas – which is thus preserved for the next generation. Three of the important ancient teachers from whom many modern gurus (teachers) claim descent are Shankara (780–812 C.E.), Ramanuja (1017–1137), and Madhva (1238–1317).

What is the guru tradition?

The system of guru and disciple has kept Hinduism alive for thousands of years, without the need for a central hierarchy or single authority. Hinduism has very little formal structure outside the network of gurus, priests, and holy people and their ashrams. These are centres of learning and spiritual practice, which are found at important holy places throughout India.

Well-established families have links to ancestral lineages of gurus, from whom they have received guidance and inspiration over many generations. Anyone wishing to be dedicated to spiritual practice will choose a guru as a personal teacher. The pupil will have to demonstrate his or her sincerity through respect and obedience to the guru, who in return will train that person in spiritual practice and in the scriptures.

All authentic gurus must trace their authority from the Vedas through the line of teachers from which they are descended.

Devotees congregate to hear a guru explaining the scriptures. The authority of such teachers depends on their having studied and served at the feet of their own teacher.

Disciples gather to honor their guru and receive his blessings. He will guide them in their spiritual practice.

Who are the sages of the mountains?

Many holy people live as recluses in India. They are known as *sadhus*. They live in caves on mountain slopes in the Himalayas, or in the depths of the forests, or on the banks of rivers. There, they practice penances and daily meditation, and teach their disciples. The history of Hinduism owes much to these teachers, who are honored above even the most powerful political figures. Their simple lifestyle, and lack of material possessions, earns them a special respect from Hindus, who understand that the highest goal of life is to be detached from material goods, and to transcend the attraction of physical comforts and pleasures. Many stories about the power and authority of these teachers, who include Vyasadeva, author of the *Mahabharata*, and Valmiki, author of the *Ramayana*, are told in the scriptures.

DEBATE - Do you need a guru?

- Yes. The guru tradition is a central part of Hinduism. It is best to learn from someone who has more experience and knowledge than you do.
- No. Today there are so many books and resources available that the idea of submission to a guru has become outdated. It is better to be self-reliant, and find your own way of thinking, than rely on a guru.

How Do Hindus Live?

Although some traditional patterns of Hindu family life are changing in the West, as more Hindus adopt western ways, certain parts of the Hindu tradition remain unaltered.

HINDUS STRIVE TO be vegetarian, to make regular visits to the temple, to pray or meditate early in the morning, to keep a shrine in the home where food is regularly offered to God, and to decorate the home with pictures of Hindu deities. Many Hindus do not smoke or drink alcohol, but this varies between households, and even between members of a family.

What does the Hindu way of life aim for?

The four basic aims of the Hindu way of life are religion (*dharma*), prosperity (*artha*), enjoyment (*kama*), and liberation (*moksha*).

Hindus believe that practicing the basics of their religion, such as being dutiful, truthful, and non-violent, will bring the enjoyment of a happy home and life's basic comforts. Other pleasures, such as music, dance, good food, and festivals, are also all part of the Hindu way of life. Once someone has found worldly

Members of an extended family make a group outing to this temple in London. Regular worship by the family, and the presence of the family elders, help to reinforce and preserve the Hindu traditions.

Grandfather and grandson worship together before the family altar at the time of the Diwali festival. In this way Hindu traditions are kept alive over generations.

fulfilment through religion, prosperity, and enjoyment, that person will realize that the fundamental problems of life remain. They are birth, old age, disease, and death. Therefore the final and greatest goal of the Hindu way of life is liberation from the cycle of birth and death.

DEBATE - Should parents and grandparents be shown respect?

- Yes. As adults and people who have experienced the wider world, they know what is right.
- No. People must earn respect by being kind, understanding, and sharing their knowledge and wisdom.

Why is the family important?

Hindus place great importance on the family and family tradition. This is reflected in the lives of the favorite Hindu deities, for instance Rama, who protected his wife Sita, and mother Yasoda, and her mischievous child Krishna.

The extended family remains an important part of Hindu society, even in communities that have lived in the West for several generations. Parents are given respect because they possess wisdom and experience. Small children are given lots of affection and freedom, and the whole family shares in their upbringing. Elderly parents often live with their married children and their grandchildren, with two or three young families living together under the same roof as their parents. The grandparents are regarded as the spiritual authorities and leaders in the community, giving stability and continuity to the tradition.

Washermen at work. They belong to a community of washermen and their sons are destined to be washermen like them. Such social restrictions limit personal freedom but ensure the stability of society.

What are the four stages of life?

The journey of life is traditionally divided into four stages, called the "four ashrams." Each ashram lasts about 25 years.

Up to the age of 25 is the student stage, for studying the scriptures and learning the practice of yoga. It is called *brahmacharya*. Next comes household life, called *grihastha*. In this stage, a Hindu is encouraged to be active in the world, to earn money, to raise a family, and to be involved in supporting the community. Around the age of 50 comes retired life, called *vanaprastha*, when the children are grown up and can support themselves. At this stage in life, a Hindu is encouraged to practice austerity, to go on pilgrimage, and to be dedicated to the service of others. The final stage, reserved only for a few, is when a person gives up all worldly possessions and all ties to the family and society. This is called *sannyasi* and is the sacred order most respected by Hindus.

What are the four varnas?

In traditional Hindu society everyone had a duty based on that person's abilities and nature. There were four main divisions of society, or *varnas*, which corresponded to the head, the arms, the torso, and the legs. The head – *brahmin* – was associated with teaching and intellectual work; the arms – *kshatriya* – with administration, politics, law, and order; the torso – *vaishya* – with commerce, trade, and farming; the legs – *sudra* – with arts and crafts, skilled trades, and manual labor.

Each of these parts of society, like the parts of the body, has a different but equally important role to play. Today this system is not so strictly applied.

This is partly because it deteriorated into a rigid caste system, which created a very unequal society. But the concept of social duty is still influential among Hindus. An important feature of the system is that spiritual and political leadership are separate.

What is the principle of non-violence?

Non-violence, called *ahimsa*, is an important part of Hindu tradition. It has been emphasized particularly by the Jain religion, which is a distinct faith of its own but is related to Hindu tradition. The principle behind non-violence is that, according to the law of karma, any harm I do to another creature will come back to me in the future. That is why many Hindus do not eat meat and are vegetarian.

Mahatma Gandhi

A famous champion of *ahimsa* (non-violence) was Mahatma Gandhi. Gandhi was an Indian politician and nationalist leader in the 1940s during India's struggle for independence from British rule. Gandhi refused to use violence against the British. Instead, he and his followers used non–violent, passive resistance, such as gathering together and refusing to disperse when ordered to do so. Gandhi was arrested many times, but his methods hastened the departure of the British, who left India in 1947, paving the way for Indian independence.

A group of students (brahmacaris) chanting morning prayers by the Ganges. They will study Sanskrit and yoga, before entering professional life or becoming priests.

Choosing a mantra

A mantra is an aid to meditation. Here are two Hindu examples:
Om (pronounced A–U–M–mmmm) – a mantra for silent meditation.

Hare Krishna, Hare Krishna, Krishna Krishna. Hare Hare,
Hare Rama, Hare Rama, Rama Rama. Hare Hare – a mantra for saying softly as a devotional prayer.

Or you can choose a favorite short prayer from your religion.

A brahmin meditating in the morning. The best way to practice yoga is at a regular time at the beginning of the day.

What is yoga?

The main methods of spiritual practice in Hinduism are the different forms of yoga. The literal meaning of yoga is "link," referring to union with God. Yoga offers a path of discipline leading to God, and can be a whole way of life.

The most popular forms of yoga practiced by Hindus are *karma* yoga and *bhakti* yoga. Karma yoga is the path of selfless service, either to other people or to God. Bhakti yoga is the path of devotion to God through prayer, worship, and service. Central to bhakti yoga is the chanting of a mantra (repeated word or sound) as a regular offering of devotion.

Another yoga path is *jnana* yoga, which is the yoga of knowledge through discrimination and study of the scriptures. *Raja* yoga, or royal yoga, is the form of yoga popularly practiced in the West, though not usually in its complete eightfold form.

What are the eight limbs of Raja Yoga?

The sage Patanjali, who lived in the third century C.E., divided the path of yoga into eight aspects, or "limbs." To practice yoga properly, means learning to integrate each of the eight aspects into your life. These are:

- *yama* moral and ethical code of practice, such as non-violence and truthfulness
- *niyama* personal discipline, such as cleanliness and self-control
- *asana* posture and sitting, so as to be alert, relaxed, and peaceful (called hatha yoga and widely practiced in the West)
- *pranayama* breath control as an aid to finding stillness and peace in the mind
- *pratyahara* withdrawing the mind from the senses so as to concentrate inward
- *dharana* concentrating the mind to be one-pointed, without any distractions
- *dhyana* meditation, the complete form of inner concentration of the self
- *samadhi* super-consciousness, or union with God.

How to meditate

Try sitting quietly for 20 minutes in a peaceful setting. Sit on a cushion on the floor, with your legs crossed, or on a chair with your back straight. Begin by concentrating on your breathing, making it deep and regular, and relaxing your body and mind. After a while your mind will calm down and naturally become focused. Then concentrate your mind on the region of your heart and begin to repeat your mantra, either in a soft voice or silently in your mind. Do this every day, gradually increasing the time to 1 hour. You will soon notice the difference in your life.

Meditating outdoors.

How Do Hindus Worship?

The Hindu tradition has always emphasized that God is everywhere, even in your own heart. Therefore worship is not confined to a temple building.

THERE ARE FOUR main places where Hindus practice their worship. The first place is the temple of the heart and mind. The body is a temple of God, and the form of God remembered in the mind is sacred. Second is the household shrine, which is found in most Hindu homes. The third is the public temple – every Hindu community has at least one. The fourth is on a pilgrimage. It is common practice for Hindus to go on pilgrimages to famous holy places, sometimes traveling great distances.

What happens in a Hindu temple?

A Hindu temple is the home of God. At the heart of the temple is a small shrine room that houses the *murti* (sacred image) of a deity, such as Vishnu, Devi, or Shiva. There may also be secondary shrines dedicated to other deities in the temple.

The main deity lives in the central part of the temple and is served by priests. In the early hours of the morning the priests "wake up," bathe, and adorn the

Sisters worship at their home shrine. Worship in the home is part of the everyday pattern of family life. It establishes a link with God through offerings of food, flowers, and incense.

deity. At intervals during the day, the priests perform the ceremony of *arati*, when they light a lamp and offer it to the deity before passing it among worshipers as a blessing. The priests also make regular offerings of food to be blessed and distributed to worshipers. In front of the deity room is the hall where worshipers gather to sing prayers or hear the teachings of the scriptures. At night, the deity "sleeps" and the temple is closed.

How do Hindus worship at home?

Most Hindu families keep a household shrine dedicated to their own deities. Often the shrine also includes pictures of their guru and their deceased relatives. Worship in the home is part of the daily rhythm of life. Food cooked in the kitchen is first offered to the deity, along with flowers and incense to sanctify the home.

DEBATE – Should people worship images of God?

- Yes. The image in the temple encourages devotion to a personal God. All the deities of Hinduism are aspects of one God, formed according to descriptions given in the scriptures.

- No. This is idol worship. Any attempt to make a sacred image belittles the greatness of God, who is beyond anything that humans can imagine.

It is quite common for the elders of the family, such as the grandparents, to maintain a regular and devout cycle of daily worship. On festival days and special family occasions, the shrine becomes the focus for the whole family.

In India, a typical Hindu temple will have a high outer wall surrounding an inner courtyard that contains the main shrine.

CANOPY

INNER SHRINE

WALL

TEMPLE ENTRANCE

MAIN PRAYER HALL

Worshipers remove their shoes before entering the main prayer hall. In front of them is the deity room. Above this is a tower or canopy, which represents a holy mountain.

ENTRANCE

Worshippers honour the deity by walking round the inner shrine. This is called circumambulation.

How do Hindus celebrate life's landmarks?

The journey of the soul through life, from conception to the final departure, is marked with ceremonies called *samskaras*. These remind Hindus of the sanctity of life and invoke divine blessings at each stage. Nowadays, only some are the ceremonies are performed.

What happens at birth?

On either the tenth or the twelfth day following the child's birth, the name-giving ceremony takes place. At the same time, the child is taken outside the house and shown the sun for the first time, symbolizing the journey from the dark world of non-being to the world of light and being.

At five months old, the child is fed grains for the first time, and when the child is either one, three, or five years old, the child's head is shaved as a symbol of purity.

Hindu rites of passage

1 Conception
2 Braiding the expectant mother's hair
3 Offering to Vishnu (eighth month of pregnancy)
4 Birth-rites (tenth day after birth)
5 Naming the child (tenth day after birth)
6 Showing the child the sun (tenth day after birth)
7 First solid food (at five months)
8 Shaving of the head (1, 3 or 5 years old)
9 Introduction to the alphabet (3 or 5 years old)
10 Initiation by the guru (12 years old)
11 Initiation into Vedic studies (12–15 years old)
12 Entering adult life (16 years old)
13 Marriage
14 Last rites

A young boy receives his sacred thread – the cord worn about the head and shoulders that denotes someone who has been initiated into the sacred Vedic wisdom.

A couple prepare to exchange their vows at a Hindu wedding ceremony. They pray to live a long life together in health and happiness.

DEBATE - Are arranged marriages a good idea?

- Yes. A marriage stands a better chance of success if both partners are chosen as suitable for one another and are supported in their choice by their families.
- No. The practice of arranged marriages is outdated. People should be free to make their own choices without any interference.

How is marriage celebrated?

Hindu marriage brings prosperity and good fortune. It is the cornerstone of community life. Many Hindu parents choose a partner for their son or daughter by arrangement with another family. If either partner does not wish to marry the person chosen, he or she has the right to refuse.

Traditionally, a husband's duty is to protect his wife, and hers is to serve her husband. At a deeper level, the marriage is a partnership of two souls who help each other to grow in love and understanding of God.

At the wedding ceremony, the couple exchange vows in front of a sacred fire. The bride says: "May my husband have a long life. May my family prosper. Let this fire make me and my husband one."

Then the bridegroom says: "Let your glory increase day by day. Let us be in good health. Let us together lead a harmonious life for a hundred years." Together they then walk around the sacrificial fire and, as they take seven steps, the bride prays to Vishnu.

What are the last rites?

At death, when the soul is about to leave the body, a few drops of water (ideally from the Ganges River) and leaves of the sacred tulasi plant, are placed in the mouth. After death, the body is washed and dressed in new cloth, then carried in procession to the cremation ground, where verses from the Bhagavad Gita are recited for the peace of the soul. After cremation, the flowers, bones, and ashes are scattered in the nearest sacred river, or in the ocean.

Pilgrims traveling through the sacred forests of Krishna near Vrindavan. Here, as a child, Krishna played with his divine companion, the goddess Radha.

The world's greatest religious gathering

The pilgrimage of Kumbha Mela on the Indian subcontinent happens every 12 years. In 2001, it attracted nearly 100 million pilgrims, making it the biggest religious gathering the world has ever seen.

Four sites are used in rotation for the pilgrimage. They are Prayaga (Allahabad), Haridwar, Ujjain, and Nasik.

India, Pakistan, Bangladesh, Bhutan, and Nepal). They go to keep a vow, to fix the mind on God, to meet holy teachers, to seek companionship, and to find inspiration.

Why is India sacred?

Hindus establish new sacred places wherever they go in the world. But they have special reverence for India. India is the birthplace of the Hindu tradition, and its great rivers, mountains, and forests figure in sacred stories associated with every part of the Indian subcontinent. These stories include the descent from heaven of the River Ganges, the exile of Rama to the Dandakaranya forest, Krishna's bathing in the Yamuna River at Vrindavan, and his construction of a great sea-fort in Dwaraka Bay. The subcontinent is full of sacred places associated with different incarnations of God and holy teachers, and is a land of pilgrimage.

Why go on a pilgrimage?

The desire to travel is a natural human urge. Historically, people of all cultures went on pilgrimages to great, sacred places. In this way, they saw the world. Only in the modern age has pilgrimage been replaced by tourism.

In India, pilgrimage is still the principal reason for travel. Every year, hundreds of millions of Hindu pilgrims travel across the length and breadth of the Indian subcontinent (which includes

What are the four main pilgrimage sites?

The Hindu word for a sacred place is *tirtha*. It means "crossing-place" – the place where the soul can pass from this world to the next. The four holy places of India are Badrinatha, in the north; Puri, in the east; Ramesvaram, in the south; and Dvaraka, in the west. Many Hindus make a vow to visit all of these in their lifetime. Three other ancient holy towns are Ayodhya, birthplace of Rama; Mathura, birthplace of Krishna; and Varanasi, which is sacred to Shiva.

What are the seven holy rivers of India?

The River Ganges and her tributary the Yamuna are sacred to Vishnu, Shiva, and Krishna. They rise in the Himalayas and flow into the Bay of Bengal. The River Sindhu, or Indus, flows from the Himalayas across Pakistan to the Arabian Sea. Three other great, sacred rivers – the Narmada, Godavari, and Kaveri – rise in southern India. The seventh sacred river is the mythical river Sarasvati, which is believed to flow underground across northern India.

A joyful group of pilgrims reach the bank of the Ganges at the holy town of Varanasi. By bathing here, they hope to fulfil many wishes, and will return home inspired and refreshed.

What is the Hindu calendar?

The Hindu calendar is a lunar calendar – it follows the moon. The 12 Hindu months are Magha, Phalguna, Chaitra, Vaisakha, Jaistha, Asadha, Shravanah, Bhandra, Aswin, Kartika, Agrahayana, Paus. Each month begins on the day after the full moon or, in southern India, with the new moon. Each month lasts 30 days, so the Hindu year is several days shorter than the solar year, which most calendars follow. To even this out, every few years an extra lunar month – Adhik – is added to the Hindu calendar.

What are Hindu festivals?

Hindu festivals are occasions for coming together, for storytelling, for praying, for singing, and for fasting or feasting. Some festivals coincide with the full moon or the new moon. The 15 days of the waxing moon are called the "bright days," and those of the waning moon are the "dark days."

The spring festival, called Holi, takes place on the full-moon day, or 15th bright day, of the lunar month Phalguna. This usually falls in March.

Calendar of Hindu festivals

Mahashivaratri (Shiva's birthday)
14th dark day of Magha
Holi (Spring festival)
Full Moon (15th bright day) of Phalguna
Rama Navami (Rama's birthday)
9th bright day of Chaitra
Hanuman Jayanti (birthday of the monkey-god Hanuman)
Full moon (15th bright day) of Chaitra
Ratha Yatra (Chariot festival)
2nd bright day of Asadha,
Raksha Bandhana (The tie of affection)
Full moon (15th bright day) of Shravanah
Janmastami (Krishna's birthday)
8th dark day of Bhandra
Diwali (Festival of Lights)
New Moon (15th dark day) of Kartika.

Food is an important part of the Diwali festival. It is a time for feasting and welcoming in the new year with fireworks.

The chariot festival, called Ratha Yatra, is in honor of Jagannath, a form of Krishna originating in eastern India. Nowadays this festival is celebrated by Hindus all over the world.

Holi is an occasion of merriment, high spirits, and bonfires. People go on to the streets and throw colored water and powders to recall Krishna's childhood play, and welcome the coming of spring.

Krishna's birthday is celebrated at the festival of Janmastami, which usually falls in August. Krishna was born at midnight in a prison house. Devotees fast all day, and in the evening sing songs as they rock a cradle with an image of the child Krishna inside. At midnight they break their fast by feasting.

Diwali, the Festival of Lights, usually takes place in October. The festival honors Lakshmi, goddess of wealth, and celebrates the triumph of light over darkness, or good over evil. On the darkest day of the month of Kartika, lamps decorate houses to welcome back the hero Rama and his wife, Sita, from exile in the forest. Their return is joyously celebrated with fireworks. For many Hindus, the following day is the start of the new year. The festival of Diwali is also celebrated by followers of the Sikh faith.

Has Hinduism Changed Over Time?

Hinduism is a very old religion and, in the past, changes within it were measured over centuries. But today it is changing more rapidly than ever before.

THE MODERN ERA for Hinduism began in the eighteenth century with the European influences brought to India by the British. For the previous 750 years, Hinduism had coexisted on the subcontinent with Islam, a religion introduced to India by invaders. For the most part, during this time the two religions did not greatly affect each other, and Hinduism changed little.

But, from about 1785, the year that the Bhagavad Gita was first translated into English, the pace of change increased.

How did the British change Hinduism?

The British army and British traders who came to India were accompanied by missionaries. The missionaries introduced Christian values and challenged social practices that they

British Hindus in Manchester are now well established and flourishing. Here they are celebrating the festival of Diwali.

found unacceptable. These included child marriage and aspects of the caste system, in particular the discrimination suffered by the so-called "untouchables." Hindu leaders responded by introducing reforms, many of which were aimed at returning to the basics of Vedic teachings.

Later, Hinduism spread abroad, as Indians living under the British Empire in India were encouraged to emigrate to other parts of the globe. In this way, Hindu communities sprang up in all the continents of the world. Whereas earlier, Hinduism had been entirely Indian, now it became a global religion.

What happened after independence?

The partition of India in1947 led to the creation of three nations: Pakistan and Bangladesh (originally West and East Pakistan), which are constitutionally Muslim nations (following the Islamic faith), and India , which is constitutionally a secular nation, which means it has no state-sponsored religion.

What is Hindu fundamentalism?

Since the time of partition, tensions between the Hindu and Muslim communities have surfaced and occasionally flared up , and a new political form of Hinduism has arisen to counter the Christian and Muslim influences absorbed in India over the previous 500 years. The new fundamentalist kind of Hinduism resists the influences of western culture and western values in India.

Rise of the BJP

Constitutionally, India is a secular nation, meaning that it has no state-religion. But the Hindu majority put pressure on the government to favor Hindu interests. This led to the formation of the B.J.P., which is now the most powerful political force in India. B.J.P. stands for Bharatiya Janata Party, meaning "the people's party of Hindu India." India's Hindus, who number some 800 million, feel that their religious and cultural identities are being eroded, while the country's 150 million Muslims feel underprivileged and threatened by the huge Hindu majority.

The magnificent temple built by the Swami Narayana Hindus in North London has become a landmark and symbol of the new British Hindu community.

Is Hinduism growing?

Hinduism has become a part of the fabric of many countries in the West, as Hindus have settled there and brought up successive generations in the Hindu tradition. As Hindu communities prosper in Europe and the U.S.A., they have built more Hindu temples, and interest has grown in preserving and expressing Hindu culture.

Contemporary Hinduism as an active religion in the West has been influenced by a number of international Hindu movements.

Who has helped promote Hinduism?

The Ramakrishna Mission was founded in Bengal in the nineteenth century by Vivekananda and named after his guru, Ramakrishna. In its monastic organization and its emphasis on welfare work through hospitals and schools, it was influenced by Christian missions in India. In the West, Ramakrishna Missions concentrate mainly on teaching meditation and Vedic philosophy.

The Swami Narayana Mission started in India, in Gujarat, early in the nineteenth century. It stressed devotion through education and community service, earning the respect of the British governors. Today it has a strong presence wherever Gujaratis have settled abroad, such as countries in Africa and the Americas, and in the UK. Its temples are often elaborate works of craftsmanship wrought from marble and stone. In the West, the Mission runs several Hindu schools.

The Visva Hindu Parisad, meaning "World Hindu Association," was formed in 1964 in reaction to the Indian government's secular policy, to promote

Students from a girls' school run by I.S.K.C.O.N. (International Society for Krishna Consciousness) perform a traditional Hindu dance at a Hare Krishna festival in England.

At Bhaktivedanta Manor near London, England, a western devotee of Krishna explains her faith to a visitor during the Janmastami festival. Every year, the festival attracts some 50,000 worshipers from the surrounding area.

traditional Hinduism in a non-sectarian way. The Association is dedicated to reawakening Hindu consciousness and fostering cooperation of Hindus throughout the world. Its emphasis is on a universal and inclusive form of Hinduism.

What is the Hare Krishna movement?

Another group that runs Hindu schools in the West is the Hare Krishna movement. It is based on devotion to Krishna as taught in the Bhagavad Gita. Although the roots of the movement are in Bengal, on the Indian subcontinent, a large proportion of its members are not of Indian origin, making it a truly international form of Hinduism.

DEBATE - Should non-Indians be able to become Hindus?

- Yes. Hinduism is based on the philosophy of the Vedas, which is universal and non-sectarian. We should be free to choose the religion that most appeals to us and inspires our faith and trust.

- No. Hinduism is deeply identified with the land and people of India. We should stick to the religion we are born into, because that is best suited to our nature.

An American woman who has converted to Hinduism joins in celebrations in a temple.

What has Hinduism given to the West?

Hindu culture, with its vibrant temples, arts, fashions, and food, has brought much that is new and valuable to multicultural societies in the West. Hinduism's informality, and the open-mindedness shown toward different religious traditions, appeals to westerners looking for greater freedom of religious expression. Hindu practices such as yoga, meditation, astrology, alternative medicines, and vegetarian health diets have attracted widespread interest.

Why are Hindu ideas catching on?

Karma, reincarnation, and other Hindu ideas are becoming widely absorbed among the informal beliefs of many people. Karma encourages us to take responsibility for our behavior and to learn from our mistakes. In today's world, when human actions affect the global environment so profoundly, "karmic" consequences are increasingly of concern to us all. Modern society encourages individual freedom, so the idea of taking responsibility for one's own actions is an important concept.

Which is the main yoga teaching?

Most yoga teachers in the UK are registered with the British Wheel of Yoga. The yoga taught is based on a modern form of the traditional teachings of Patanjali, modified to suit western needs. Its philosophical basis is found in the Hindu scriptures, but the emphasis is on the physical exercises, called hathayoga, rather than on the spiritual practices of yoga.

Where is more traditional yoga taught?

The Self-Realization Fellowship, founded by Paramahansa Yogananda in 1920, teaches yoga as a basis for meditation. The Fellowship has several offshoots, with centers in most major cities around the world. It aims to teach meditation techniques that lead to peace within oneself and an awareness of God's presence.

Why is TM so famous?

T.M., or transcendental meditation, is practiced by some 5 million people worldwide. It became famous when, in 1965, the popular music group the Beatles travelled to India to meet its founder, Maharishi Mahesh Yogi. While there, they stayed at his ashram in the Himalayas.

Partly as a result of the Beatles' great popularity, T.M. rapidly spread across continents. Today, T.M. broadcasts go out every day of the week via a network of eight satellite channels. The broadcasts include education programs to teach science, technology, and healthcare according to the principles laid down in the Vedas.

Why is yoga special?

Yoga, with its emphasis on personal transformation, offers people a proven way of enhancing their own lives through exercises and routines that anyone can learn and practice. There are many organizations, originating within Hinduism and now extending beyond its traditional boundaries, that offer guidance and tuition in meditation and yoga.

The pop group, the Beatles, meet the Maharishi Mahesh Yogi. This highly publicized meeting brought transcendental meditation into the limelight.

What is the Hindu view of vegetarianism?

Hinduism teaches that all creatures are God's children. All life is sacred because the soul can be incarnated into any life form, so animals should be treated with care and respect. There are karmic consequences for inflicting suffering on other beings. We should treat all creatures – human or animal – as we would wish to be treated ourselves, Hindus say. For these reasons, a high proportion of Hindus are vegetarian.

Why is vegetarianism good for you?

The yoga tradition stresses the importance of a healthy diet. It divides foods into three kinds: those giving vitality, those creating disease, and those causing tiredness. The human digestive system, it says, functions better on a balanced vegetarian diet. Compared to meat and fish, vegetarian foods tend to be low in fat and high in fiber. Vegetarian food is also safer, because it contains much lower levels of chemical additives than does meat.

As well as being healthy, vegetarian cooking can also be very tasty. There are many good vegetarian cookery books on the market, with lots of delicious recipes to try.

Why is vegetarianism good for the world?

Hindu tradition is against eating animals, not only because it is considered cruel and unnecessary, but because it is wasteful of the earth's resources. Fattening animals for slaughter uses up valuable grains that

Sadhus, Hindu holy men, happily share their encampment with two cows. To Hindus, cows and humans deserve equal care and affection.

Vegetarian food is served at a Hare Krishna festival. The food has been blessed with prayers, to show that all food is a gift of God.

could be fed directly to people, especially in poorer countries. The big herds of animals favored by modern farming also require the large-scale clearance of land, a heavier use of chemicals, and the production of more polluting substances. All this is against the Hindu tradition of small-scale, humane farming.

How does vegetarianism help your mind?

A vegetarian diet, according to yoga philosophy, adapts the mind to more subtle and sensitive vibrations. This, in turn, produces greater spiritual awareness. The violence involved in a meat diet, and the karma that this creates, coarsens both the mind and the senses, making it more difficult to attain spiritual awareness.

DEBATE - Should experiments on animals be allowed?

- Yes. The suffering of the animals is for the greater cause of helping us overcome suffering by developing new medicines. Human beings are a superior form of life to animals, and so we have the right to take their lives in an attempt to benefit our own.

- No. We do not have the right to inflict suffering on innocent creatures. We should find other ways of conducting medical research. All creatures are God's creation and all have an equal right to life. If we inflict pain on another living being, we will ourselves suffer a reaction.

What is Hindu medicine?

Hinduism has its own complete system of medicine. It is called Ayurveda and is thousands of years old. Ayurveda recognizes three basic "humors" that regulate the body and mind. They are known by the Sanskrit names *vata* (wind), *pitta* (bile,) and *kapha* (mucus). They correspond to the elements: *vata* is a combination of air and the ether; *pitta* is a combination of fire and water; *kapha* is a combination of water and earth. When these three humors are in balance, the body is healthy, but when one or another of them is in excess, this causes disease.

Each of us has a constitution that belongs to one of these three types, Hindus say. The balance of our health can be maintained by eating and living in accordance with our individual type. Ayurvedic treatment is based on the use of herbs and diet to correct any imbalance in a person's constitution.

Why is Hindu medicine so popular?

Ayurveda is gaining ground in the West as part of the trend toward alternative medicine and a move away from the powerful drugs prescribed by modern medicine. Drugs can often create imbalances in the body, not cure them.

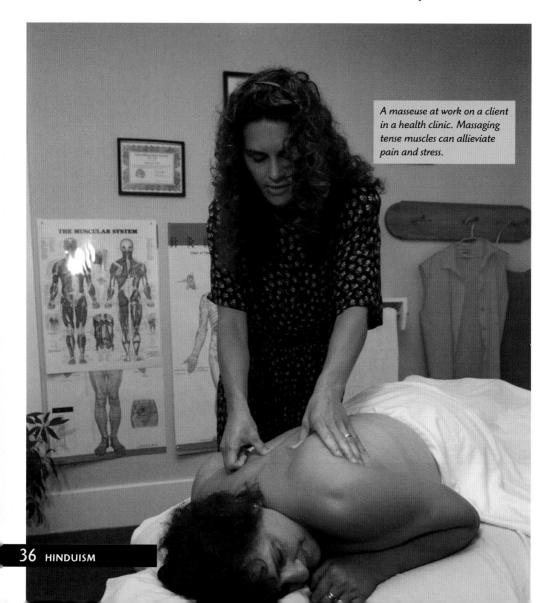

A masseuse at work on a client in a health clinic. Massaging tense muscles can allieviate pain and stress.

The essential characteristic of Ayurveda, which makes it different from ordinary, conventional Western medicine, is that it stresses prevention as the key to good health. By living and eating in a healthy way, and with regular exercise and good habits, you have a better chance of not falling ill.

Ill health, says Ayurveda, has three main causes: negative emotions, for instance anger or fear; eating too much food, or eating the wrong kind of food for one's constitution; and lack of personal hygiene. Ayurvedic cures are based on herbal remedies, massage, and cleansing diets, as well as changes in lifestyle, yoga, and meditation to calm the mind.

What is a yoga cure?

Health farms, which are popular in the West, are a largely Hindu invention, originating in traditional yoga cures. On a health farm, patients follow special diets with a routine of exercises and massage in a stress-free environment. In India, many middle-class Hindus visit special yoga clinics, where they are restored to good health by cleansing their bodies and minds through yoga diets and exercises.

DEBATE – Can Ayurvedic medicine help us in the West?

● Yes. Ayurveda keeps your body and mind healthy through exercise and a healthy diet. That way, you won't need expensive drugs to restore you to health. Treatments based on Ayurvedic cures are safer and cost much less than many modern treatments. They can also complement modern medicine.

● No. Ayurvedic medicines are scientifically unproven and outdated. They are ineffective and we should not place our faith in them.

A herbal medicine store in India. The use of herbal medicines is widespread in the East and is becoming increasingly popular in Europe and North America.

What Challenges Do Hindus Face Today?

Traditionally, the Hindu way of life has been based on the extended family. Today, in the West, that pattern may be changing along with other traditions.

IN WESTERN COUNTRIES, young Hindus who go off to university mingle in an environment quite unlike the one they have been used to, where people live their lives differently. After university, many young Hindus never move back into the family home. They start a new way of life modeled on the society around them. Others, who seek to retain their Hindu cultural roots, find new ways of expressing them. As a result, new forms of Hinduism are emerging in Europe and North America.

Will the Hindu family system survive?

It is normal for there to be tensions between generations. But these are magnified when children grow up in an altogether different society from the one that nurtured their parents and grandparents. This is the case with the second and third generation of Hindu

An older Hindu couple in Britain maintain their traditional way of worship at home, seated on the floor with no need for furniture. Such traditions are rapidly changing.

At their local temple, two young children receive tuition in Gujarati, their mother tongue. Much of their religious and cultural tradition is passed on through language.

The best of both worlds

Research has shown that children growing up in Hindu families, but within the host culture of a western country, are often well equipped to take advantage of the best of both worlds. This helps them find stability in their lives. That is why Hindu family traditions can be expected to remain strong and healthy, even though family behavior may change in response to new social patterns.

immigrant families in the West. Even Hindu marriage is changing, with divorce, which in traditional Hindu society is almost non-existent, becoming more accepted among Hindus in western countries. Yet, despite outside cultural and social pressures, the Hindu tradition of obedience to the authority of parents remains strong.

What about other cultural traditions?

A key to cultural continuity is language. Most Hindu families living in the West have kept their mother tongue, which preserves many of their religious and cultural traditions. That language may be Gujarati, Punjabi, Hindi, Bengali, or one of the many other languages native to India. Efforts are made to pass on the language to younger generations by means of special classes held in temples and community centers. But despite this, outside India traditional languages are gradually falling out of use.

Another tradition is the sari, a long, silk or cotton wrap-around dress, worn by Hindu women in India. In the West the sari is becoming less common among Hindu women, as they conform more to western fashions. But many will still put on a sari to visit a temple, for festival celebrations, or to attend a social occasion such as a wedding.

What links are there with Hindus in India?

Most Hindus in the West have family and community ties back in India, and as they prosper they are able to help their ancestral communities, financially and with social support. A challenge for the future will be to maintain and strengthen these ties, which are beneficial to both Hindu communities and to the world at large.

What is it like in the West as a Hindu?

Many Hindus growing up in the West feel uncertain of where they fit in. This is especially true of those from religious homes, where more liberal moral and social habits are frowned upon. Often there is a lack of understanding about Hinduism in society, even among some young Hindus. Although they may visit Hindu temples and join in with their festivals, many of them lose touch with basic Hindu beliefs and teachings. But others are showing signs of a desire to explore their cultural roots and learn more about their faith.

Do Hindus encounter prejudice?

When Hindus first settled in the West, they lived mostly in inner-city areas, where they met with prejudice. But as they became more established in the wider community, the prejudice diminished. Today they are part of mainstream western society and are active in all walks of life. Within the Hindu community itself there is sometimes prejudice between different social groups. Some tightly knit immigrant communities still resist intermarrying, or even mixing socially, with people of other faiths.

New identities for young Hindus

Among Hindus, there is less resistance to mixed marriages than there used to be. For the younger Hindu generation in Europe and North America, these are liberating and exciting times. Young Hindus are mixing more outside their own community and defining new identities for themselves as western Hindus.

An immigrant Hindu makes a living in England by maintaining an age–old religious tradition. He reads horoscopes and Hindu scriptures in order to advise Hindus in his community how to conduct their lives.

Two of the main actors in the musical Bombay Dreams, *which has popularized Hindu culture and brought "Bollywood" film sets and costumes to the London stage.*

Do Hindus permit drugs and alcohol?

Usually, among Hindus, it is only the men who drink alcohol. But habits vary from one community to another, depending on factors such as caste and cultural background. Drugs are generally regarded as harmful to mental and physical well-being. In India, some sadhus who worship Shiva smoke cannabis, but this tradition has not made the habit acceptable to the general Hindu community.

What are Hindus' views toward sex?

In the Hindu tradition, sexual restraint is valued as promoting health and a long life. Sex outside marriage is strongly discouraged. Perhaps because of this, Hindus do not seem to recognize the existence of gay men and women. Even in the West, issues concerning homosexuality are not debated openly in the Hindu community. For these reasons, education about A.I.D.S .and practising safe sex faces obstacles in traditional Hindu society. And partly as a consequence, India is now facing a serious A.I.D.S. epidemic.

DEBATE - Are mixed marriages wrong?

• No. All people are God's children. The marriage of people of different faiths enriches life and society.

• Yes. Intermarriage can lead to both partners giving up their religious values and, if they have children, failing them on religious education.

A banyan tree in a sacred grove among the forests of Krishna in Vrindavan, India. Beneath the tree is a small shrine dedicated to the spirit of the tree.

How do Hindus care for the environment?

Hindus revere rivers, mountains, forests, and animals as sacred, and love to be close to nature. Many Hindu villages have a sacred lake, surrounded by a grove of trees to catch rainfall and protect the banks of the lake from erosion. Together the lake and the trees store water for irrigating the fields and supplying the wells in the village with drinking water. Not only are such landscapes serene, but they also serve as habitats for wildlife.

Unfortunately, in recent times these simple techniques for gathering and protecting clean water have been neglected. This has led to serious water shortages and, in many parts of India, to the spread of desert land. Hindu practices of caring for nature are being forgotten, making human survival in this environment more difficult.

Do Hindus believe in a simple life?

In Western society, success is measured in terms of possessions, while people follow a lifestyle that consumes more than the earth can afford. This has been

Hindu teachings for the modern world

Vandana Shiva says three Hindu teachings stand out in today's world:
1 All people of different faiths are your brothers and sisters.
2 Do not take more than you need. As Mahatma Gandhi put it, "The earth has enough for everyone's need, but not for everyone's greed."
3 We all have the capacity to take responsibility for our own lives and to be teachers and leaders by our personal example.

called "high living and simple thinking." By contrast, Hinduism teaches the value of a simple life. Living simply, Hindus say, keeps us closer to nature and to God, bringing more happiness. All the world's religions agree that the highest standard of life is the simplest. This is known as "simple living and high thinking."

What do Hindus think about G.M. crops?

One of the world's best-known campaigners against genetically modified (G.M.) crops is the Indian scientist Vandana Shiva. She is motivated by her native Hindu beliefs to stand up for the rights of rural women and farmers. She fought against the genetically modified "terminator" seeds – seeds that produce only one crop, forcing farmers to buy new seeds each year from the suppliers.

She also campaigns against companies trying to patent (claim the sole rights to) the sacred Neem tree. Hindu stories tell of how this tree came from a drop of

A farmer rides placidly to work in the fields in the early morning. The traditional simple way of life is highly valued in India, but it is also changing fast.

divine nectar carried to earth. Neem provides a natural and harmless alternative to pesticides (pest-control chemicals), but multinational business corporations have tried to patent it for their own use.

DEBATE – Do Hindu values apply to helping the planet?

- Yes. Every single person who acts with conviction can make a difference.
- No. The problems are too great for anyone acting alone to be able to make any difference. We are powerless to change the way the world is.

How do Hindus look after the elderly?

The overall attitude of Hinduism toward life and death is one of acceptance rather than struggle. Old age and the gradual decline of the body as death draws nearer are not necessarily seen as being bad. Old age brings wisdom and the opportunity to devote more time to prayer and spiritual practice. In Hindu society, elderly people command an authority and respect that provides an important anchor for the community. They are treated by everyone with a great deal of affection.

What do Hindus think of death and dying?

For Hindus, there is no taboo connected with death. When death comes, it is allowed to happen as a part of the inevitable cycle of reincarnation.

When someone dies, their remains are cremated as soon as possible, to help the soul let go of the dead body and continue on the journey of reincarnation and spiritual growth.

Traditionally, Hinduism is opposed to suicide, although sometimes people did deliberately end their lives by fasting in a holy place. In the debate over euthanasia – mercy killing – Hindus

DEBATE - Should you have to look after your grandparents?

- Yes. Grandparents deserve respect and it is a privilege to look after them.
- No. The state should provide care for the elderly. They have earned it by working, paying taxes, and possibly fighting for their country in the past.

A Hindu family photo: three generations closely linked.

A Hindu women working in a watch factory workshop.

believe that nature should take its natural course, without interference either to prolong life or to hasten its end.

Do Hindu women have equality with men?

Today, it is not unusual for women to be major Hindu religious leaders. For much of the twentieth century, Anandamayi had a large following throughout India. More recently, teachers such as Mother Gayathri, in Britain, and Nirmila Devi, in the United States, have risen to prominence. One of India's most famous politicians was also a woman. Indira Gandhi was twice India's prime minister, but was assassinated in 1984, during her second term.

How were women treated in the past?

Historically, Hindu social customs often disadvantaged women. These customs included child-marriages, in which

Women's rights

Today, in India, women's rights are an important issue and many of the old, unfair practices are being swept away. However, as in most parts of the world, men remain dominant in public life.

young girls were betrothed to much older men; the practice of *sati*, when the widow was expected to join her dead husband on his funeral pyre and burn to death (though this seldom happened); polygamy, which allowed a man to have two or more wives; and the dowry system, which required a young woman to bring a substantial gift of money or land to her future husband.

What does the future hold for Hinduism?

Hinduism is a very ancient religion, with a philosophy that dates back at least 3500 years, and possibly much longer. It has stood the test of time, and still inspires 850 million of the planet's population. Although the world changes, and people's lives change, the essential teachings of Hinduism will remain much the same as they have always been. That is Hinduism's strength. Its fundamental truths have been relevant to generations down the ages and still are today.

Hinduism in the future

Future generations will see a significant change in Hinduism. From being a religion confined to a particular race of people and a particular land, it will shift across the globe to become a religion that belongs to peoples of all races and all lands. This change is bound to produce a flowering of new ideas and new ways of expressing Hinduism's ancient truths.

An English convert to Krishna consciousness, who has adopted the traditional Indian sari. As she brings her children up in the Hindu faith, she must wonder how they will express their own beliefs, and what role they will find in the world.

A Hindu celebration in a garden in England – where East meets West.

Will India's influence grow in the world?

It has been said that the twenty-first century will belong to India and China, the two most populous nations on earth.

Unlike China, India is a democracy, meaning that the people elect the country's leaders. In terms of population, which is still expanding, India is the world's largest democracy. But India's economy lags behind those of Europe and the U.S.A. For India to sustain its economic growth and provide for its vast population, Hinduism's ecological traditions will need to discover new ways of using the country's natural resources.

Much of the environmental crisis facing the planet today is due to the way that people in the West live their lives and use up valuable resources. We may all need the softer influence of eastern faiths and cultures, such as Hinduism, to restore the delicate balance between nature and the way that is used to serve human needs.

Will Hinduism blend with western life?

As Hindu families settle in the West, they establish their own social and community networks. Their children put down roots in their adopted countries, and become part of mainstream society. Many of the younger generation are going into commerce and business, or are being drawn into caring professions and becoming doctors, teachers, and social workers. Others prefer working in the arts or the media, and some are entering the world of politics and government.

They bring to their professions a subtly different approach to life to that of their colleagues. Through them, Hindu world-views are entering mainstream society in Britain, North America, and Europe. As they prosper and become more successful, their influence will grow. In the future, Hindu ideas of spiritual equality, of non-violence, and of the virtue of simplicity will become more accepted and shared by more people.

REFERENCE

Numbers and distribution:

The world total of Hindus is estimated at 750 million, of whom 700 million live in India. In earlier periods, India had her own links throughout southeast Asia, where Hindu merchants settled in Burma, Malaysia, and Indonesia. Under the British, Hindus were encouraged to emigrate with the British Empire to Mauritius, British Guyana, Surinam, Trinidad, South Africa, and to countries in East Africa. After 1945 they mostly emigrated to Britain, the Netherlands, U.S.A., Canada, New Zealand, and Australia.

The map above shows those countries of the world where Hinduism is the dominant religion – only India and Bangladesh. The map below gives details of the Hindu population in countries in southern Asia.

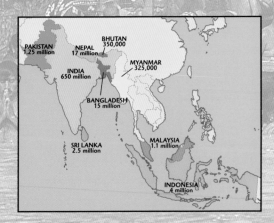

PAKISTAN
1.25 million

NEPAL
17 million

BHUTAN
350,000

MYANMAR
325,000

INDIA
650 million

BANGLADESH
15 million

SRI LANKA
2.5 million

MALAYSIA
1.1 million

INDONESIA
4 million

THE DEVELOPMENT OF HINDUISM

3000 B.C.E.	According to ancient traditions, Krishna speaks the Bhagavad
2000-1000 B.C.E.	The first Vedic hymns are recorded in Sanskrit
200-300 C.E.	Patanjali writes his Yoga-sutras, dividing the path of yoga into eight aspects
780-812	Shankara founds Advaita, the impersonal school of Hinduism
1017-1137	Ramanuja establishes the Vaishnava devotional tradition in South India
1020	Islamic forces enter India under Mahmud of Ghazni
1370-1440	Ramananda, with his follower Kabir, combines Hindu and Muslim teachings
1469-1539	Nanak, influenced by Kabir, founds the Sikh religion
1486-1533	Caitanya teaches the Vaishnava devotional movement in North India
1785	Bhagavad Gita first translated into English, by Charles Wilkins
1869-1948	Mahatma Gandhi, who led India to independence
late 1980s	Hindus settle in countries dispersed across the British Empire
1893	Vivekananda represents Hinduism at the World Parliament of Religions in Chicago and goes on to found the Ramakrishna mission
1947	Indian Independence and partition of the subcontinent into Pakistan and India
1960-2000	Hindus from India and East Africa settle in Britain, Australia, and U.S.A.
1964	Foundation in Delhi of Visva Hindu Parisad, the World Hindu Association
1965	The Hare Krishna movement appears in New York
1972	Hindus are forced out of East Africa and settle in Britain in large numbers, other Hindus emigrate to U.S.A.
2001	The world's largest ever religious gathering, Kumbha Mela at Allahabad, attracts 100 million Hindus.

HINDU HOLY PLACES

Rivers:	The four special places:	Pilgrimage towns:
Ganges	Badrinatha – in the north	Ayodhya – birthplace of Rama
Yamuna	Puri – in the east	
Narmada	Ramesvaram – in the south	Mathura – birthplace of Krishna
Sindhu (Indus)	Dvaraka – in the west	
Godavari		Varanasi – sacred to Shiva
Kaveri		
Sarasvati (the hidden river)		

The Six Major Faiths

HINDUISM
Founded
Developed slowly in prehistoric times

Number of followers
Around 850 million

Holy Places
River Ganges, especially Varanasi
(Benares). Several other places in India

Holy Books
Vedas, Upanishads, Mahabharata,
Ramayana

Symbol
Aum

JUDAISM
Founded
In Canaan (modern Israel and its
neighbors), possibly around 2000 B.C.E.

Number of followers
Worldwide about 13 million

Holy Places
Jerusalem, especially the Western Wall

Holy Books
The Torah

Symbol
Seven-branched menorah (candlestick)

CHRISTIANITY
Founded
Around 30 C.E., Jerusalem

Number of followers
Worldwide around 2000 million

Holy Places
Jerusalem and other sites associated
with the life of Jesus Christ

Holy Books
The Bible (Old and New Testaments)

Symbol
Cross

ISLAM
Founded
The formal religion was preached by
Muhammad starting in 610 C.E. in Arabia
(modern Saudi Arabia)

Number of followers
Worldwide more than 1000 million

Holy Places
Makkah and Medina, in Saudi Arabia

Holy Books
The Qur'an

Symbol
Crescent and star

SIKHISM

Founded
North-west India (now partly in Pakistan), fifteenth century C.E.

Number of followers
Worldwide 16 million

Holy Places
Amritsar in India

Holy Books
The Guru Granth Sahib

Symbol
Nishan Sahib: swords and a circle

BUDDHISM

Founded
535 B.C.E. in northern India

Number of followers
Worldwide 360 million

Holy Places
Bodh Gaya, Sarnath (both in northern India). Many other places of pilgrimage

Holy Books
The Tripitaka

Symbol
Eight-spoked wheel

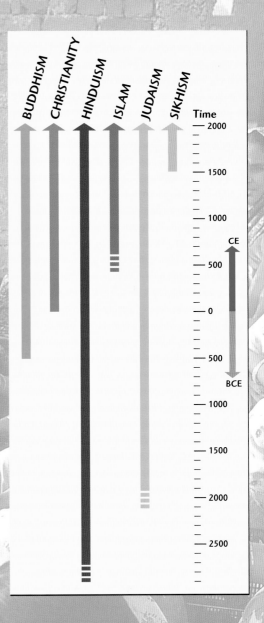

BUDDHISM CHRISTIANITY HINDUISM ISLAM JUDAISM SIKHISM

Time
— 2000

— 1500

— 1000

CE

— 500

— 0

— 500

BCE

— 1000

— 1500

— 2000

— 2500

While some faiths can point to a definite time and person for their origin, others do not. For example, Muslims teach that Islam predates Muhammad and goes back to the beginning of the world. Hinduism developed from several prehistoric traditions.

GLOSSARY

Glossary of key Hindu concepts with their Sanskrit terms

atma The self: body, mind, or spirit; or the Supreme Spirit.

avatar "One who descends," one of the ten forms taken by Vishnu on earth.

Bhagavad Gita "Song of God," taught by Krishna, the best-known spiritual teaching of Hinduism.

bhakti Devotion to the Supreme Lord.

bhaktyi-yoga The path of devotional service to the Supreme.

Brahma The first created being, created by Vishnu; the grandfather of the universe, member of the Hindu trinity.

brahman Spirit; the pervasive presence of the Supreme; the Supreme.

brahmin Teacher or priest in traditional Hindu society.

caste Rigid division of Hindu society, often leading to discrimination.

deva Divine being; the higher order of created being.

dharma Universal religious principles; essential quality that unites all beings with the universe and with God.

guru Teacher of Hinduism, in the traditional "disciplic succession" system.

Hanuman Monkey-god, son of Vayu, god of the wind, in *Ramayana* epic.

Hindu Follower of Hinduism, derived from name of River Sindhu (or Indus).

japa The soft or silent repetition of a mantra as prayer or meditation, may be counted on a japa-mala, a string of prayer beads.

jiva The individual soul, hence jivatma.

jnana Knowledge.

jnana-yoga The path of knowledge of the Supreme.

karma Action; past actions, which accrue results; hence can refer to the results of past actions.

karma-yoga The path of dedicating actions to the Supreme, thus gaining freedom from the consequences of action.

Krishna The eighth incarnation of Vishnu, creator of the universe, and teacher of the Bhagavad Gita.

Lakshmi Goddess of fortune, who accompanies Vishnu.

Mahabharata Epic story of India, in which Krishna teaches the Bhagavad Gita, the "Song of God."

mantra (*man* "mind," *tra* "release" in Sanskrit) A spiritual sound vibration on which to focus the mind and the senses.

moksha See *mukti*.

mukti Salvation; liberation from the ties of karma and the cycle of rebirth.

Om The sacred sound – made up of three letters, A-U-M – representing the Supreme Truth and said to be the sound from which the universe was created.

Paramatma Supreme Self, or Supersoul, who dwells within every living being.

parampara The system of disciplic succession, or lineage of spiritual teachings.

Ramayana Epic story about the divine king Rama and how he rescued his wife, Sita, and devoted himself to his people.

reincarnation Being reborn in a new body.

sadhu Saintly person.

samadhi Mystical trance; complete absorption in the Supreme.

samsara The seemingly endless cycle of birth, old age, disease, and death.

Sanatan Dharma "The eternal truth of life," the traditional name for Hinduism.

sannyasi A member of the homeless order of celibate monks.

sastra The Vedic literatures; authoritative religious text.

sat Truth, reality.

Shiva The form of God who dissolves the universe with his dance in a circle of fire.

varna The four main divisions of Hindu society.

Veda Spiritual knowledge; the ancient Sanskrit hymns directly revealed by God.

vidya Cultivation of knowledge; education.

Vishnu Preserver of the Universe, who creates the universe from his breath, and Brahma, the first living being.

visvarupa Universal form of God, as pervading the whole universe

yajna Sacrifice, an offering to God as a form of worship.

yoga Link or union, usually the relationship between the soul and God; a spiritual discipline seeking closer union with God; one of the six Vedic philosophical systems.

yogi Someone who practices yoga.

FURTHER INFORMATION

BOOKS and MAGAZINES

An Introduction to Hinduism, Gavin D. Flood, Cambridge University Press, New York, 1996

Hinduism, Klaus K Kostermeir, Oneworld Publications Ltd, 2000

Hinduism: A Very Short Introduction, Kim Knott, Oxford Paperbacks, 2000

The Sacred Cow, A.L.Basham, London, 1989

Science of Self Realisation, A. C. Bhaktivedanta Swami, Bhaktivedanta Book Trust, 1975

Am I A Hindu?/The Educational Primer, Ed Visvanathan, Halo Books, 1992

The Heart of Hinduism, Rasamandala Das, ISKCON Educational Services, 2002

Teach Yourself Hinduism, Hemant Kanitkara, W Owen Cole, V P Kanitkara, McGraw-Hill/Contemporary Books, 1996

The Illustrated Bhagavad Gita, Ranchor Prime, Godsfield Press/Barrons Educational Press, 2003

PLACES TO VISIT

In the United States:
The Hindu Temple of Greater Chicago
10915 Lemont Rd,
Lemont,
IL 60439
tel (630) 972-0300
Two traditionally-designed temples combine together to be one of America's best-established Hindu centres of worship.

Ramakrishna-Vivekananda Center of New York
17 East 94th Street,
New York,
NY 10128
tel (212) 534-9445
The main East Coast centre of the Ramakrishna Order of India. The centre has a library and bookshop, and is open Sundays, Tuesdays and Fridays.

Sri Venkateswara Temple
Pittsburgh
1230 South McCully Drive,
P.O. Box 17280,
Penn Hills, PA 15235
tel (412) 373-3380
The South Indian style temple, located in Penn Hills east of Pittsburgh, is one of the earliest Hindu temples to be built in the United States, begun in 1976.

Vedanta Society of Southern California
Hollywood Temple,
1946 Vedanta Place,
Hollywood,
CA 90068-3996
tel (323) 465-7114
The temple was established in 1929, and its origins can be traced back to Swami Vivekananda's visit to Los Angeles in the late 1890s.

In Canada:
Sri Bhuvaneswari Temple
746 Warden Avenue, Unit 10-11
Scarborough, ON M1L 4A2
tel (416) 615 0005

Murugan Temple
1611, St.Regis Blvd,
Dollard-des-Ormeaux, Quebec
H9B 3H7
tel (514) 683-8044

WEBSITES

www.hindu.org/temples-ashrams
Provides a list of Hindu temples in U.S.,
Canada, and worldwide.

**www.bbc.co.uk/religion/religions/
hinduism**
Basic objective information from the
British Broadcasting Corporation.

www.hindu.org
General Hindu databank.

www.hinduismtoday.com
Hinduism Today is a global magazine
service to the family of Hindu faiths,
produced by a small Shaivite (Shiva
orientated) monastic community based
in Hawaii.

www.iskcon.com
The main web-site for the Hare Krishna
movement.

www.krishnatemple.com
Complete and user-friendly web-site of
Bhaktivedanta Manor, one of England's
most popular temples.

www.ramakrishna.org
Home of the international Ramakrishna
Mission.

www.ramatemple.org
Informative web-site of The Hindu
Temple of Greater Chicago, one of
America's pre-eminent Hindu temples.

www.swaminarayan.org
The home of the main international
branch of the Swaminarayan Mission
(Bochasanwasi Shree Akshar
Purushottam Swaminarayan Sanstha).

www.tirumala.org
All about one of South India's most
famous temples.

ORGANIZATIONS

American Hindu Association
P.O. Box 55405
Madison, WI 53705

Balagokulam Centers in U.S.
1225 Vienna Drive 929
Sunnyvale, CA 94089-1866

Vydic Yagnya Center
P.O. Box 28613
Santa Ana, CA 92799

American Institute of Vedic Studies
P.O. Box 28613
Santa Ana, CA 92799

Hindu Temple Society of Canada
P.O. Box 424, Station 0, Toronto,
Ontario, M4A2N9

INDEX